healing happens

Michelle L. Tate

Copyright © 2012 Michelle L. Tate

Cover Art by Deanna Minich

All rights reserved.

ISBN: 147957570
ISBN-13: 978-1479157570

One of the most gifted healers of all time once asked me,

"how is the wound the healer?"

I have nothing to gain by sharing this heart-guarded response. Perhaps I have only ego to lose.

Gratefully, I go ahead into this unknown place of question.

With each uneasy step, some universal voice.

The wound itself is also the healer…whenever and however we allow it to be.

Wound.   Healer.

Haven't we all been this and that?

Ultimately, it's all about love. This I know is true.

CONTENTS

	Acknowledgments	iii
1	JH	1
2	Remodel	7
3	Barely Hanging On	15
4	Consumed	23
5	To Be Heard	26
6	Hollow Space	29
7	Start	31
8	Homesick Simmered	33
9	Warrior Angel	36
10	Life Evolving	41
11	Memory Lanes	44
12	Overhaul	47
13	Union	51
14	Matter of Time	65
15	Across Stages	75

16	Feel	79
17	Belief	81
18	Boat Ride	84
19	Council of Warriors	96
20	Heard in Silence	100
21	Healing Yet	112

ACKNOWLEDGMENTS

Immense gratitude to my Mom, the most courageous warrior of us all. She does not do what's easy, and not always what others would call "right." But <u>every</u> day, she does *something*, out of love unconditional for her children. My Mom is brave like that. If I could do anything great in this lifetime, it would be to make for her at least one day in which she could allow her own precious self to come first.

Thank you to my family, friends and amazing teachers. I could not be who I am today without you. Special gratitude to Kimberley for getting me started with my first journal.

Thank you to Jim, for supporting and encouraging all of what I do, through every single day. Strength of many, with a childlike wonder that never ceases to amaze and inspire me.

Lisa, for all of what we do to experience and touch this life, I remain deeply enriched, encouraged and inspired. Since our meeting my personal journey has become ever more remarkable. I continue to be grateful for you and what we share. Thank you for what you do for us, always.

John Honey. Thank you. I wonder, how does it feel to launch a forgotten fleet? Without you, is not a thought worth having. Shine on brother, shine on.

VS, thank you for helping me untangle, and for helping me to realize that a safe place isn't only found outside.

My thank you list could go on forever, and so it will. Deepest love to you all. For the time you have taken to touch my life, a grateful heart remains.

Universal Nod.

The cover art for this book has proven to be as rich an experience as any.

Found the image on the internet - loved it.

Lisa, whose fantastic role in my life is beyond description, began the daunting task of finding its original creator, as the image itself is found on many business and personal websites, Facebook pages, blogs, and various sites both nationally and internationally.

Of the many possibilities, she chose to contact three.
Two of them did not respond at all.

The one who did respond is indeed familiar with the origin of the image.

She is, in fact, the gifted artist of this very brilliant painting and a most wonderful person.

With extreme graciousness, Deanna Minich has allowed us to use her artwork on the cover of this book.

Some might call this simple coincidence.

Some others of us might consider it
                a sort of universal nod.

I have no idea into whose hands this book will fall.

But wherever it lands,

    I begin to truly believe,

                      it is meant to land there.

JH

Sing to me your song
relaxing me with music
freeing me from me

how is the wound the healer?
waits for some response, from me…

patient doctor
grateful for you,
 through all things
  even through my shelled-up-self

simplicity can answer
as can logic
but with no feeling behind the words
 I find myself unable to produce them

they fall away before being born,
  from me

what *is* being born from me?
no great, original thought
nothing you haven't heard throughout many lifetimes
nothing that hasn't been said for years before these

nope, nothing here inside my walls to offer…

and so, I close my eyes or look away

the best I can do is
 offer some….something…
  without words that are so common

here, language is communication

because I have no words
       to label
             what it is I feel

   does not make it any less real

like heaven

you asked whether or not I believed in heaven

I said yes,
    immediately - question to myself

       what is it?   heaven?

no words to describe it

my understanding of heaven is
    not a line of up or down
         comfortable or uncomfortable
           good or evil

heaven…is the description and the word itself.

so what is it that I lost?

I watch a person struggle
with insecurity and fear

I feel for that
and do what I can,
       to comfort.

anything to comfort,

because human life is so damn hard.

>　　　so is human death.

I catch a glimpse of myself
>　　　　　　　in the mirror

when will I recognize that person?

when will I love her?

I say, "now." "forever."

...how often must I do this
>　　to make it so?

how do I do this?

I do not understand how to do this.

I wonder if you have become as tired of me
>　　as I have become of myself.

Challenge.

I don't know if things have become too easy for me,
>　　or if I have become too simple for most things.

tend to believe the latter...
>　　leaving me empty inside.

what is gone from me

    was supposed to have gone, unnoticed

        yet I notice the gap.

this is what I hear
in a whisper

this was not for you to hold
it was only moving through

this memory was not meant to become
your chemistry…let go, let go, let go

how can I not be confused?

recognition of sound before it comes forth
taste, before it reaches my tongue
'real' memory of what is not 'real'

at night, unable to sleep

silence is actually quite loud

      ironic

so, there is a sound to silence too…

you are no better than me,
so you say

an argument we will have

forever

things have not been
challenging enough for me

hold some passion
show emotion

real.

just a word.

REMODEL

this knowing I know
has killed me and betrayed me
wiser to go free

a child, peeking out from behind a stone hedge,
> not sure.

Is it to protect me from you,

 or me from me?

Why can't I believe you could love me?

fear of not being loved to the depth of my own.

Unfair of me to judge that you do not own this depth,
I know.

So let me put you over there, away from me.
> For your safekeeping.

The source of abounding joy and relentless pain, together as one.

It is like hanging, ripped open,
from a barbed wire fence.

not sure I want to drop,
  not sure I want to climb back over the other way,
    not sure I want to be anywhere.

> but still,
>> I am here.

Torn flesh and outsides
> wearing what once was my inside.

I don't even feel like covering it up anymore.

Is it good or bad?

I don't know, it just is.

I am hanging here, free and open
 for all the world to see.

The ones who recognize both me and this state
    advise – "hang on or let go."

Hm. While others are hanging here with me,
   too tired, like me
       to care much about anything
         or anyone right now.

Like me, they sense
  this is a battle of life and death.

 trying to grab hold of reins
    that are just out of
        disjointed reach

teasing,

                flapping in the wind.

I am watching.
tired of reaching.

wonder what will come now that
    I have decided to

        wait   it   out.

There is a lesson here somewhere.

 I will not leave until it comes.

now looking all around,
    upside down,
           sideways,
    backward,
           forward.

Notice others' movement.

Free of this,
free of themselves,
free of knowing they are even alive.

Does that make them dead? They look like it to me.

I wonder, when it comes to be "time" for them,

   what will they be thinking?

                    wishing?

                           missing?

Nothing? Makes me sad to these bones.

Why should it?

I am not them…
           or am I?

Even those strangers to me,
  are somehow on my list of favorite people.

Where the hell did I go?

What is it about me,
 that does not want you to come any closer?

This is a different story to write,
  but I am understanding here,

> from behind these tears,

the shell of armor I wear

is wearing pretty thin.

Turns out it was not made to last for centuries.

This empire all *around* me, is not me.

I thought it was to protect and keep me whole.

It is not.

I have been locked in,
        just as others have been locked out.

Thought I had full control of the drawbridge.

Beginning to realize that
I don't always work it well.

it is lonely in here.

I have been touching hands through windows,
   hearing conversations through walls,

letting myself dissolve into
no relationship with myself

but into dream and some memory.

At first, I didn't doubt what I was seeing,
hearing,
 knowing.

     some hollow breeze within.

I am convinced now.
I am in the wrong place,
at the wrong time.

I become quiet and begin

      solitude.

I learn that I allow entrance,
 deciding who comes and goes.

I know every nook and cranny.
I know every dusty corner
and every hidden trap door.

Can watch you head toward
any of my secret hiding places,
        can keep them just out of your reach.

        This is my castle.

Turns out there is no king or no queen,
    I have left it to be managed by the wind.

Busy, looking and loving to the outside,
    enjoying the inside
        without understanding
            the need for me to be
                in love in there, too.

What I've not prepared for,
 are those who don't want to come in,

but instead invite me out into their world,

 where there are surprises
        and lack of control
        and silliness
            and things to happen
                beyond anyone's plan.

Still, I like to go it alone.

Can be in the company of others,
    just not too far into that company.

I have created isolation,
    and I have come to love this.

Today I learned,
that I have also come to hate this.

 ~ right now,
    the drawbridge I am stuck to
            is eating me alive.

It's everything I built

    right down to the barbed wire

        clawing at my flesh.

...today I learned,

    it's time to remodel.

Barely Hanging On

Watch the autumn fall
talk with leaves that meet the earth.
Fearlessly, they die.

There are times I feel like

I am

    barely

        hanging

              on.

Like a spider hanging from a new spun string.

Looking up at the star
who had just cast me out
      and down to the
           circular concoction below.

I am too big to land there.

Even the blues and the greens cannot hold me.

  - that gray movement,
that blur surrounding that space
doesn't appeal to me at all.

The silence I am hanging in,
           is thick…like black custard.

The vibrations above me are exhilarating and hot.
White Hot.

I want to go up, not drop.

I want to return to that spot,
   right there behind that big as life flower.

It was really wonderful there.
Start to pull myself back up.

Rope begins to sway.
I am getting that sinking feeling again.

The fiber between my liquid-like fingers
begins to get warmer.

Understand without words that soon it will be fire.
Pleading, I look up.

There is someone peering at me
 from behind the dark purple petals.

a soft, beautiful man
quietly moving into view now.

This movement
  is not movement
    as I know it in my body
        hanging on.

it is…gliding.
      icy, smooth,
flowing.
beautiful to me.

I remember it.
I miss it.
I miss him.

Envious and excited,
  begin to climb up again.

He puts his toe, which is wrapped in what looks like
some silken sock just near the base of my rope.

>   I am quickly becoming
>   much
>   smaller.

Doesn't stop my desire or demand to return.

I try to move faster - before what is coming, comes.

He is smirking. It pisses me off.

"For you," he says,
   just before he puts his toe
      to my thin rope of hope.

Green hot flames shoot from the base
 and down to my grip.

falling now at speeds that make my eyes flap,
ears scream and brain want to explode.

In the free fall, I am fighting
to watch him through the flames
that are now turning
to ice chunks around me.

"Better to watch where you're going," he says.

Turns his back on me and disappears
behind my flower.

I look down in just enough time to see the pin-point
hole I am destined to come through.

Plummeting through,
eyes closed, teeth clenched.
        It is like being sucked
              into a watery,
                            winding,

compliantly
                tight-fitting

   tube.

Somewhere between there and here,
some memory lost.

But it is

Warm and Quiet.

I am resting, buoyant in some fluid
that supports me here now.

Lingering here isn't so bad,
was even nice for a moment.

Begin to fidget. What's next?

        I'm getting bored.

I hear laughter behind me and turn
like a fish in a bowl to see who I've heard.

 "Already?"

He brushes past me and I follow his flow,
feeling his presence span our distance with ease.

His robes are layered and multi-colored.

He has come to sit with me here.

His smell is of the incense that I have come to love in this life, and his thickness is of fresh, clayish earth.

   Makes me feel at home and at peace.

"When you were there, you cried to come here. Now that you are here, you cry to go there."

"I want to go back with you," I say.

His eyes become like sapphires that
blaze a maze through me.

One hand comes forward.
 - tips of his fingers rest at my forehead.

as though he is melting into my flesh
                which isn't really that just yet.

as though he is *adding* himself to me.

I am hearing, feeling,
    tasting, smelling,

    being

what I imagine is love.

Through all of the memories
and all of the dreams
and all of the births
and all of the deaths,

there has been love.

Through all of the ugliness
    and all of the disaster
        and all of the chaos
            and all of the war,

there has been love.

From a different space, I understood that.

From here, it's different.
        I forget that here.

I get lost here.

"You are not getting lost. You can only get lost if once you knew the way," he says.

"You've been there, running here. You've been here, running there.
>   Until you can be there and *be there*,
>   and until you can be here and *be here,*
>   you will continue in this way.
>   It is not *getting lost*.
> It is *not showing up* that's slowing you down."

He is getting ready to leave and I am getting ready to panic.

Plead my case one more time.

I don't want to be here all alone.
There is nobody here like me.
I have been searching and searching
for words that match mine,
thoughts that spur mine,
voice that inspires mine,

for comfort that reaches to this depth.

Even for a flower that
remotely resembles my flower.
the color alone would be some relief,
but they don't make that color here.

As he walks away, he looks at me over his shoulder.

Ignoring my fears and their cry,
he raises one hand that silences me.

"That color," he says, "is everywhere. You only have to open your eyes and *see* it."

CONSUMED

Take from me, movement.
Becoming still, I observe.
You and I are one.

I need to find balance again.

What is it about my personality that makes me give so much away?

CONSUMED

I've been burying myself here further and further,

        deeper,

                deeper

can still see the light?

better go

        deeper.

Am I building a warrior or a coward?

The warrior finds balance.
The warrior is true.
The warrior moves from love and pure intention.
The warrior, is still.

The coward knows no balance.
The coward runs fast and hard,
moves big and loud.

The coward, will crumble.

will never last.

I can be a warrior.

I believe I will be.

I have met the coward.
She moved in for a while.

I didn't like her and she didn't like me.
She didn't stay long.

<u>Once it has been, it is known.</u>

Good or bad,
it cannot return
in that first way again.

This is where I touch it lightly and let it go.

Grateful for the event,

    whatever it was

        or was not.

To Be Heard

*Comfort, go from me.
With you here, I cannot learn.
You blind me from truth.*

Ego screaming to be heard.

"There's nothing special about you," I say.
"Be quiet, settle down. Go away."

"Why? Why? Why? Why? Why?"

"Because they say so!
They're telling me!
I'm paying a high price for you
and your noise! Shut up!"

P U L L I N G

 ripping

inside swallows me whole.

Outside is *so very* loud.

                        bewildered.

                                              i am lost

Frozen.

    I can barely move.

...it takes all I have
        to stand under the weight
                of your voice.

Ego rising – "relax,"

        I whisper.

It only wanted a hug.

"you are special," I say.

    ...why can't I breathe?...

there is something eating me from the inside out.

Hollow Space

Before the mirror
I stand, one question in hand.
Who is looking back?

Finally moving in here
 after lots of other places

finally looking at me
 after lots of other faces

Feeling every part of me
wrap around the moment of the moment

other knowledge won't release me
 though I've never freely shown it

this body needs me

little baby frightened, crying
watching from a step ahead

coming in to wear the body
   matching up

did it hurt?

I don't know…

    let me see your eyes

   they'll tell me what my reaction should be.

START

*Gently now I glide
to the truth of who I am.
i do not exist.*

I have been praying
for some healing

for as long as I
remember.

What made you think
it would be easy?
asks Universe.

Where else could we start
if not with you?

Your prayers have been
answered and continue to be.

Nobody said it would be easy.

Homesick Simmered

have I brought some joy?
then my spirit, she may dance
happy, every step

Know what I saw the other day?

A billion rainbows before we named 'em,
layered deep, could almost touch 'em,
Sun rising, setting, dawning, resting,
calming waters, need no testing.

Moon to balance daylight's falling,
Stars to answer heaven's calling,
a waterfall, a perfect storm, a sea
of peace surrounding me.

Forests filled with life unending,
beings living, not pretending,
shining, glowing, softly showing
love as it was once worth knowing.

Know what I heard the other day?

Music I've not heard for ages,
compiled across many stages,
every pitch and every tone,
a melody so close to home,

harmony of angels blending,
delighted by the joy their sending,
every language making sense
all allowed without pretense,
a blend of now and once and past,
a song I pray will last and last.

Know what I felt the other day?

A warming breeze across my cold,
a letting go of what I hold,
an embrace I haven't felt for lifetimes,
rest throughout my sleepless night-times,
trust that said I could be free
to drop the cloak that covers me.

Homesick simmered,
defense thinner,
resting here for one short moment,
enough to ease the quiet torment,
believing I could be believed,
softly, parts of soul retrieved.

Wanna know where all this happened?

    Right there...

           in your eyes.

WARRIOR ANGEL

*Armor is heavy.
Instead I choose a feather
to guard this ego.*

Let it go
It's awesome I know

He connects me to my pillar
that connects me to the light

In comes my age old friend

    "Well, here we are."

"It's good to see you," I say.

    "How can you say such a thing?"

I do not understand the question.

He smiles at me with the glimmer of heaven.

    He is my warrior angel.

He folds his arms across his chest and I find myself doing the same.

"How can you say what is good to see? You appear to be blind to this life."

I look around and see my history.
Our history.

I see people, suffering and lost.
Makes me sad and mad and blind.

Frustrated, I ask,

"Why don't you *do* something for them? Why are you here, wasting time with me? Look at them."

"No. I am looking at you."

Well then, let me call them over.

And here is your cancer,
your headache, your torn heart.

Wish I hadn't taken the heartbreak,
        this memory, wait…that's not mine…

Is it?

"Look away then," I say to him.

"No. I am looking at you."

He cocks his angel head and says,

"Look closer.

WE ARE EVERYWHERE.

~ but I belong to you.

And I am going nowhere.

I am looking

        only

            at

                you.

I love you."

that is talking to my star
that is coming through the pillar
that is connecting me to light of light
of earth of earth

no matter where I dig to hide,
the eyes do not fall away

They are on me,
   with me,
      loving me

Someone once told me I didn't need this
   confusing the part of me that likes it
      meeting those who felt without it
         releasing mine so they could find it

angel warrior rests by me
doesn't take his eyes off me
kills me with this love for me
I close my eyes but still can see
      his image here,
           in me, in me.

Tears flow from his angel eyes
wings drape down, soft now, he cries

I watch him, filled with awe.

I touch the softness
in his heart, feel each tear he sheds.

Honor him, I honor him
    so in awe at the sight of him
        so in love with the way of him.

I close my eyes to what stirs inside.

"No," he says, "let go…"

Trust is born here.
    Faith his born here.
        Life is born here,

body dies again.

Quiet now.

So quiet now.

standing here
    on the other side

        there's something new

            ~ alive ~

Life Evolving

Quiet grows the mind
Quiet brings the soul her sight
Give to her your eyes

Life evolving to the days
    where friends
        begin to lose
            parents

Life evolving to the days
    where questions
        come a whole lot
           easier than
                answers ever
                  did

Life evolving to the days
    where seeing isn't
        nearly as precious
            as
                touching

Life evolving to the days
    where defense isn't
        nearly as powerful
            as
                feeling

armor visits from time to time
                but does not stay

I'm more concerned
                that it stay away

    especially when
        I'm wide awake
            and walking

Life evolving to the days

    where I am

        learning

            to be me

                in the days

                    of life

                        evolving.

Memory Lanes

The sky opens up.
Can you see forever there?
This is who we are.

I take a walk down
my memory lanes
before too long
the interest wanes

not just one
just one too many
not so softly
most are heavy

my choice, my way
my thought, my day
help me, help me,
which way, which way

I do not want to lose sight of you

I'll take your hand

you take mine too....

want to line up

right here with you.

there is such thing as give and take,
of course there is, it's no mistake,

but here there is exchange of one
from you to me to the moon and the sun.

I've never left you, feeling empty
never left you, feeling lonely
for every piece of me I offer,
you have met it,

made me softer.

Imagine that.

A warrior. In full armor.

Every weapon intact,
including the ones I've earned...

standing here,

    before you,

        offering you a thorny rose.

Thorns,
 to appreciate her full beauty.

I love you.

    ~ without my armor.

        I do love you. ~

Overhaul

What good is your work
If I do not do my work?
I will not waste you.

While you were in there
fixing what needed fixing,
you seem to have knocked something loose.

You see,
I'm shaking when I rise above the surface
these days,
    but I used to be able to fly
        with the seagulls
            out across the lake
                and even further.

Used to be able to disappear out there,
but my engine must be set at too low an idle now,
    because I just can't seem to move on
        or out or even ahead.

It's not like being stuck in neutral,
    'cuz I'm hitting the gas and it's got *some*
        movement…
            it just doesn't work like it used to.

My wipers used to keep my vision
a lot less blurred, but now,
    everything I see is wearing a shadow.

Keep rubbing my eyes and cleaning my glasses, but that
doesn't seem to be making the difference.

I think maybe they need to be replaced with the ones
that set aside all I do not wish to see;

you know, the ones that make sure I can get to
wherever it is that I'm endlessly rushing.

See, all this stuff piling up
    in my sights is beginning to bog me down,
        seems I can barely make it around the
            block without hesitation these days,

    and the lack of speed – I don't know,
        it just doesn't suit me I guess.

Oh yeah, and something happened
    to my sound system too.
        I used to be able to turn up the volume
            on the outside here,
                and it was really great 'cuz

    I got to pick and choose how
    much I wanted to hear.

It was all right here at my fingertips.
Worked like a charm.

Do you think you could put that back for me please?

I'm not sure what caused it,
but no matter how loud I crank it these days,

it can't compete with what I'm hearing
from out there, beyond those clouds.

I know the body isn't much to look at,
and I guess the interior might need some work,
    but it serves its purpose.

Sure it's got a couple of dents and scratches
from some hard travel,

    but it's still pretty sturdy I think.

I mean,

    as long as you don't touch the heart,

            it runs pretty good.

So maybe you could take another look,

    'cuz I think you might have

        knocked something loose.

UNION

*I give you the rights
to do anything you can
to help me go free.*

Quite a walk the other day
Met some people along my way
who swore they knew me inside and out
didn't stop to ask what that was about

I wandered off into the trees
Looking up, rooftop of leaves

quiet,

    peaceful,

        sang to me

closed my eyes so not to see

Sometimes vision makes me blind
in the darkness I can find
the way to you, the way to me,
the way back when I was the tree.

My parts have been separated along the way
thought I'd come back and get 'em someday,

quite the walk I had that day.

"What parts on you are cold?"

Looking down at my body,
    hearing some language
        I've never heard before,
            only knowing it settled
                    and made me warm.

Could barely hear you anymore.

And I didn't like that body.

It actually seemed foreign to me
    from where I perched,
        comfortable,
            away from limitations and pain.

Didn't want to come back.

"I can't name them."

I didn't care what they were – that pile laying there,
pathetic and worn out,
    not even strong enough to cry.

From here, I can wrap myself around the universe.

I don't need those arms or those hands,
    I can do it all from right here.

Who needs those feet?

From here, I can rest myself on the moon and beyond.

I've got quite the view of all the world.

    and from here, I can't feel a thing.

        heartbreak is just a story.

I'm separate from her here.
Separate from her arms and legs
    and heart and parts,

and I don't really care what you do with that frame.

I'm digging it right here.

Watching, I see her try to fly.
    She's reaching, stretching…

I can help her, but I don't want to live there.

Wonder why doesn't she ask me anyway?
I don't understand her.

Look at what she puts her body through.
Look at the saint who repeatedly
works to put her back together.

She is so full of fire that she wants to be consumed.
She should be careful what she wishes for.
Sometimes, I am tender toward her.

I reach down from here and hug her.
She barely takes the time to notice.

But I can't be with her there and be here too.
It matters there to her,
on a large scale.

Here, it means nothing at all.

which should I listen to?

On the one hand,
this means everything there is.

On the other,
nothing more than a blinking eye.

Even her eyes are tired.

I've tried to stay there, in that suit with her,
but she keeps kicking me out.

That body and I don't seem to want to fit,
though she really is quite beautiful.

It's too bad.

My body is dying again.
I somehow know the feeling.

I was so close this time,
to what I believed was a reunion.

I see her there, watching.

Can't blame her for staying away.
I haven't figured it out yet.

I hear your voice.
I pay attention to "my body"
and what it's feeling.

What is it feeling?

Like a snake that has shed
his skin and then tried to re-fit it.

I am struggling.

This is not easy, nor is it comfortable.

This skin is much too tight,
    and inside
            is
        cold.

Not Chicago-winter cold,
    that would be warm in comparison.

Cold that is even inside my teeth,
inside each bone,
    inside each vein,
        inside each cell,
            and inside that too.

COLD.

I relax my jaw, try to keep my teeth
from chattering as I try to name the parts.

My body, is trembling

no wonder she checked out.
No wonder she is sitting there,
    away from me.

I imagine I am quite the sight right now.

My throat is filling with something
and my ears are ringing
and I cannot make this body
fit what I'm feeling the need to do.

Is there any warmth at all?

Pinpoint. Right below my navel.
a speck of orange, sunset orange.

Trying to get to the center of it.

I am thankful for you and your voice,

I get easily lost in here.

I might have missed it there…

I wonder how often I have missed it before,
though it's always been there.

I am bathing in it now,
body is beginning to thaw.

Maybe once, this relief was enough.
To get even this far, was enough.

But I still see her there,
untrusting me.

This relief is no longer enough.

I want to go further.

I wonder how I can get her to come back…

Again I hear your voice,
 as though someone is feeding you my thoughts.

Could it really be that easy?
Can I really just reclaim her?
Trusting completely. I will try.

Parts that I left in the universe, come home.
Parts that I left in the care of strangers, come home.
Parts that I turned my back on in fear, come home.
Parts that I disrespected, come home.
Parts that I left in the dreamworld, come home.
Parts that I left in death, come home.
Parts that I left unattended, come home.
Parts that I didn't love, come home.
Parts that I didn't admire, come home.
Parts that I let get too big, beyond me, come home.
Parts that I buried in the dirt of the earth, come home.
Parts that I left on the expressway that night, come home.
Parts that I left on the railroad tracks, come home.
Parts that I left abandoned, come home.
Parts that I haven't let die, come home.
Parts that I left in the river, come home.

Parts that fled from criticism, come home.
I will be more kind to you, no matter what.
Parts that I fed to some ego, come home.
I will accept you, no matter what.

Parts that left because they couldn't be seen,
come home. I will see you, no matter what.
Parts that I pretended not to hear in every silence,
come home. I will listen to your voice, no matter what.

I have not loved you
or even respected you in the way that I should.

In your humanity, your divinity, your insecurities, your
fears, your worries, your love, your compassion, your
goodness, your desire, your lust, your wanting, your
wishing, your bad thoughts and good thoughts, come
home.

I will love you, no matter what.

That's it. That's my plea.

I wait for not even a second and
my crown becomes like a wishing well.

I am feeling, even seeing
    orbits of light coming in from the
        top and vibrating
            down through my body to my feet.

It becomes color somewhere near my heart,
maybe just a touch lower,
it is a shade of green
that I cannot quite define.

Below it begins brilliant hues of yellow,
and deep sunset orange,
even shades of red
cascading like a waterfall
into the soles of my feet.

Before I am lost in this feeling,
I wonder, "Where is it coming from?"

It is no longer enough just to know this feeling,

I am looking for the source
                            as a source;

not just an amazing, wonderful surprise.

 I have
experienced a connection to a star.

It came down and fed me
then danced me into some bliss
that set me free for those hours.

Returning was difficult and
left me lonely where I sat.

I have never been the same again.

But the aching state it left me in
   made me never want to go back.
               didn't do well with the return.

I have not been back there since.

some new voice is talking to me.

A faceless form of yellow light – not clear,
                         but radiant, sunshine yellow,
                                    sitting here with me.

Is it her? Has she come back to be with me again?

The voice is not feminine or masculine.

I have never heard such a sound,
telling me about this form sitting beside me.

                "This is your Self. This is your being.
                      Is it wonderful?"

I am in awe.
I cannot believe such a thing.

Surely that is somebody else.
    I cannot hold such brilliance and beauty
            in this simple frame.

"It is not so simple at all," I heard.
"It is a priceless gift, to be cherished and treasured and honored."

The being glides to what I assume are feet.
            it is standing now.
                It is crackling and vibrating
                        and putting out warmth and a chill.

I can hear it.

"Hands" are extended before me,
palms facing me,
inviting me.

I am standing before it now,
  with a feeling of being on the edge of everywhere,
        nowhere, and every place in between.

As I offer my hands up,
I feel extraordinary power before I make
     contact.

For an instant,
I am afraid I may not be able to handle it.

For an instant, I stop.

Thankfully, fear dissolves.
nothing left but invitation.

I rest my palms against this light.

the feeling is hot and cold and
     alive and healthy and
          abundant with love and energy.

It is peaceful and harmonizing
     and soothing and calming and
          nothing shy of sheer bliss.

It is, I think, pure love.

"Are you here to protect me?" I ask.

Without an answer,
I feel this sensation of something I still
cannot describe,

        But I try.

it is vibrant, nurturing, powerful,
    forgiving, unconditional, infinite love
        entering the walls of my skin and skull and
                              bones.

We are immersed in one another.

unforgettably amazing.

An answer came.

"I am here," I heard,
"because you called me home."

In disbelief,
I am standing perfectly still, waiting.

We have merged.

I am together,
 but alone, in silence right now.

It is like a dream, but I am awake.
I am somewhere in the middle.

Mirrors appear.
one before me, one behind me,
two to each side. surrounded by them.

I find myself doing something
I can't recall *ever* doing before.

> I am actually looking at my miracle.

>> I am admiring what I see.

>>> I am fascinated by what I see.

>> I am seeing….me.

> I had no idea I looked like this.

I am humbled,

> for perhaps the first time, by

>> my

>>> *self.*

Matter of Time

Sun, inspire me.
Moon, offer me your wisdom.
Show me how to shine.

When the visions began
I picked up my pace
scrambled and ran in search of a place
where I would fit in and wouldn't fall out
wondering what this all was about

as they told me of some history
that I could taste and feel and see

But others said it can't be so
we'll show you how your life should go

You should not see that native man
who tells you of his stolen land
who tells you that you once were his
how they took you too and let him live

you were never his child as he claims
and ignore what he says about no one to blame

There's always some fault and
there's always some wrong
the only good way is to stay hard and strong

all that stuff is in your head,
after this life, you're only dead

...oh.

He says they took me from his arms
he wished he'd die to spare my harm
He says the way I love that tree
is how I should be loving me

if he had been there, I would see
that I am him and he is me.

he's always been here, never been far
and he says he knows why I so love the stars

They tell me no voice comes like that
without the proof it can't be fact

So these visions then are just my mind
I'd better move quicker to leave them behind
'cuz they can't be true, they've told me so
I'm better off to let them go

The harder I run, the faster they come
telling me that it can't be undone
and I shouldn't be wasting such precious time
trying so hard to leave them behind

"You are a Warrior of the Divine,
you'll realize this in a matter of time."

Warrior?   Me?

Nope, you must be mistaken
'cuz this body's not armor and
my heart's always breakin'

the wind is enough to move me to tears
and the things which "aren't real"
are my greatest of fears

The memory of you breaks my wings and my stride
I can't tell you how many times I have cried
at the sight of a butterfly on a sunny day
trying just to make her way
across a row of flowers for hours and hours
sharing with me her unyielding power

perhaps she's the warrior that you are seeking,
but it sure isn't me 'cuz this body's still leaking
with yesterday, and yester-year and all they say I cannot hear
    or touch or taste or smell or see

        no my friend, it isn't me.

The native elder says to me,
your eyes know *more* than what you see
your heart is wise beyond your years
take the time to shed your tears
And now you'll take another step
do not carry such regret
for being born into that form, realize
you're not alone

you will find teachers on your way
in spite of what the world will say
and you must follow what unfolds
unless you choose to deny your soul

In which case it would be a shame
but *still* there is no one to blame
    you'd just become another shell
    sleeping through all sorts of hell
        unaware, oblivious,

        unattached and not concerned,
            pockets lined with dollars earned

If that's the life you wish to lead,
go on, go on - you will succeed.

I'll have to leave you, understand
and that would be a change of plans,
my hope is that you'll take his hand,
who's helping you to learn to stand
in the truth of who you are today,
the truth of who you are always,
one who carries a torch of love,
sent direct from the heavens above

take it, be it, trust it, feel it
let him help you, he can see it.

That torch - is *that* what's setting me on fire?
Making me hotter and sicker and drier?

First looking at me, then at the ground,
his voice came across with a softer sound
"…when you were my child taken from me,
the fire they lit was your ancestry.
It can no longer hurt you,
it already has – I'll walk with you through it,
take hold of my hand…"

"This lineage is not the one you read of in books,
it began before time, you dream how it looks,
in your inner most mind, in your inner most heart,
the beauty you give it, that's where we'll start."

His eyes show tears of worlds gone by
I take his hand and start to cry
as he walks me through the days I'd missed
he gives to me a precious gift
of memory, of childhood, of life and then of death,
swallowing, I realize, if this were my last breath
we could walk these paths together
and perhaps his tears would end,
"No," he says, "it's not the way,
this life you can't pretend. You must gather up
your knowing and come forth to who you are,
go on - continue living here,
just don't forget the stars.
Your home is always watching,
but you cannot do the same, yet when you need to cool
the fire, put palms up – touch the rain.

Remember that you're made of more than only flesh
and bones – some may not consider this, but that's the
stuff just here on loan.

One more journey we should take
before the choice is yours to make,
come with me just one more moment,
before I leave you to your torment,
which really is the way you choose,
not knowing what you stand to lose."

He walked me to the end of time,
and asked me if I'd stand in line
for one more lesson he was giving
to help me understand my living

Grateful for the offer now,
I'm hopeful he will show me how
to accept the terms which I've been given
and touch this life that I've been losing.

"What have you seen in this life you've lead?"
he asked of me,

here's what I said

Living well, but isolated
observing what we've all created,
loving shallow, not too deep,
struggling when not asleep

'cuz they said I was giving much
wondered who could stand my touch
of what I truly had to offer,

"she has a different way about her"

this is what I often heard,

they wouldn't understand the words
that came to me before this birth
that talked to me of life on earth

Swore myself to secrecy,
guess it didn't have to be
a solo walk through memory,
stashed away for none to see

When I touched lightly, souls would tremble,
come forth how? They don't remember
how to move beyond these limits
how we set ourselves right in it,

how these walls are made for climbing,
how we should be re-aligning.

Years continue in this place
begins to show upon my face

I cannot touch or love for real,
they do not know it – cannot feel

I do the best I can to conceal
that I see more than what they call real,
and these visions I've tried for years to hide,
please help me help them not be denied.

Can you help me see what I should be trying
that will not leave me broken and dying?

He reaches down and gathers up earth,
hands it to me in part of his shirt,
along with a stickpin, a branch and some water
saying to me that I am his daughter
he raises his hands and prays to the wind
and the fury of nature seems to begin
to whirl all around us, with no fear implanted

 - he asks me if I think I can stand it

Gently, he takes hold of my hand,
and weights me down as though with wet sand

"The words you have shared here
they cannot end here,
you must find another
to help you uncover
the magic of your mystery,
heart must open - trust me, you'll see
we'll stay right beside you,
will never deny you,
and when you are ready
you shall become steady
and you will move forth now
and soon you will learn how
to live in your being,
still see what you're seeing
without reservation or some hesitation,
live here and there,
it can be done – you've asked for guidance,
now it has come.

You've know him many years before,
lifetimes, yes – but why keep score?
It's just the human parts of you
that want to know 'just what to do.'

I'll tell you now, there is no answer
no reason not to take the chance here
your prayers have been calling
as you watched this world falling
apart and away, "heal us," you'd say

well, I'm telling you now. today is the day.

Where else to begin, if not with you?
He knows your step, he's been there too,
and no one said it would be easy,
lying there, torn up and queasy,
understand there's work to do,
he's here to help to see you through,
but understand that all you do,
begins, and lives, and dies with you.

No more child, can I say,
that's quite enough for you today,

I feel you stirring, nervous, crying,
rest a while, no more why-ing,
your meeting him is not by chance,
it is not simple happen-stance,

he too,
    is a Warrior of the Divine,

as you will be,
in a matter of time

              and those many others
                      standing in line?

    We'll get to them too.

                    Just a matter of time…

Across Stages

Does it hurt?, they ask.
No, it's magical I say.
Learning is endless.

Coming back to life again

There's always been this light of lights
surrounding me and all my sights

    Curious by darkness

Hooks set on me,
    coats and pieces,

covering me and the light I see

Those in the light
disrobed me of those,
but some I liked 'cuz they
    shielded my heart

        and gave me a barrier

      to keep me from breaking

I ask for them back
but they no longer fit
and I try to squeeze into this fear-drenched
label like it once owned me

and I swear I know better
than to close my eyes to what I just saw

Let it go, let it go…

    so I do and I will.

Looking at the eyes upon me
crying at my lifeless body
rushing off to feed me air
doing all to keep me there

someone said I might not make it
learning then just how to fake it

I remember lives before this

forms unlike this

Funny how they worry so
Like the choice is theirs if I stay or go

God intervenes with his angel, me,
asks me what it is I see
that makes Him feel this heavy heart
this sorrow that was not a part
of our plan for me and my return

close my eyes as my Mother burns

her blue eyes clearly through my being
calling me on what she's seeing
asking me to stay a while

God didn't warn me about her smile

They give me a name and take me home
it isn't like the ones I've known

before this jump, before this ride
before there was a different side
of warriors and darker places
by this time I'd be off to races

prepared for a battle
that's killed me for ages

    chasing down life across many stages

This time perhaps
    I'm a bit less ready
        as visions creep in and make me unsteady

not used to being slowed to the speed of light
I'm afraid it's not such a pretty sight

I learn that there are limitations here

held together by flesh, not fear

The spirit holds the flesh to the bone
making this my castle, and also my home

there was a chase of some piece missing
    or perhaps
        some peace missing.

Anyway.

        Precious Renovation, going well.

            Truly going well.

Feel

My eyes are busy.
What would I do without them?
What then would I learn?

Why is it that when
I walk past you,
I feel what you're wearing?

Where you've been,
  what you're hearing,
    what your noise is.

What right do I have to know
this about you?

Who are you to me?

Why do I know your mother
when I look into your eyes?

Why do I feel your death?

What right do I have to know
this about you?

My eyes burn from the inside out.
The fire gets worse with any thought.

Soon, there will be too much steam
for me to see.

…maybe that's my hope.

Belief

What does this give you?
Silently, I look around.
Isn't this enough?

When I was "just" a single cell,
I used to ask God…

    "Do you think I could ever be one of those?"

Looking down at our earth, at a newborn red ant.
    Awesome to me.

"Of course you can," he said.
    "You are special. I love you."

I dreamt big with God.

He said it, in spite of my not believing it.

We've been through many lifetimes
    and endless iterations to get me to this point.

    Every lifetime and every return,

God says to me….

"Of course you can. You are special. I love you."

Isn't that great? He just keeps

        sending me

            back through…

In this life, you are one of the first to have reached
 some part of me
  that somewhat heard you when YOU said,

  "You are special. I love you."

I came by to thank you and heard you say those
    very same words to someone else.

….that I can walk away and still hold a shred of
belief…perhaps there's been some progress.

Boat Ride

*Pausing, I wonder
is my desire too much?
My ego says yes.*

There are things I wish I didn't see.
Interactions, outer actions, inaction.

All of each connecting us,
making your decisions our shared fate.

Maybe that's why I wish I didn't see.

"We're all in the same boat?"
Well shit. I don't want to be in this boat.

This is not the line I meant to stand in.
I meant to be in that other one –
the one where beings protruded as light,
where manifestations of light and vibration and color
were everywhere…free and in love.

This boat is making me sea-sick,
rocking around with no clear direction, maybe no
direction at all.

I gain footing on a slippery, wet wooden plank
just long enough for someone to push me over again.

They pass by, oblivious to the storm clouds just over-
head and seemingly unaware of the winds picking up.
The imbalance is my fault too, of course,
because I'm looking up and to the sky when I should
be looking all around.

Still, I can't get used to this motion, and
the crew and I don't seem to work together all that well.

They keep asking me to help them row,
but they don't like when I ask where we're going.
They seem irritated by the question and are satisfied
just for the movement.

I'm not. I'm a little uneasy about our lack of
destination.

There are some really rough waters up ahead and
nobody wants to look.

…we're heading straight for them…

I don't think this ship can survive the battle.
Nobody else seems to care.

There are times they ask me to help them bail water,
usually when it has risen too high to ignore.
I say there must be a leak and we should look for it,
they don't want or like the suggestion,
they just want me to bail.

I'm beginning to think that might not be
    such a bad idea.

There are others who go on all around us,
without a care in the world… unconscious of the effort.

They're the walking dead maybe.

Eyes dull and filled with nothing,
    but they walk and talk
        like they have life.

They'll answer any question I might ask
but their words are like their eyes,
            hollow, distant, empty.

Meaningless to me.

Why does that leave me lonely?

I don't think I like these people.
They don't care about a purpose or our route.
They don't care about the weather or the sea.
They don't care what we do along the way.
All they want to do is row or bail.

So finally, I do.
I bail.

There are these smaller boats surrounding ours,
with one, sometimes two or three passengers on board.
They are looking at us from time to time,
and they see me looking at them.

I have seen others abandon this ship and go to them,
but I've never said a word about it – nobody else here
seems to be able to see them.

I'm somewhat afraid of what they might do to me if
I talk of what I see.

Some part of me understands that
the ones who have been locked up down below –
those are the ones who have either seen what I am now
looking at, or have touched what I am about to do.

Someone has invited me aboard.

A stranger to me up close
but one who has been rowing alongside this ship
for the duration of its existence. Mine too.

He looks safe to me.
There are no words between us
    but I understand all of
        what he does and does not say.

"Come on," he says. "Jump. I'll catch you."

He's waiting for a moment but I know he won't wait long.

Someone not too far from me has stopped rowing and is watching.

Maybe if I don't go now, that person will take my place.
Maybe he is just watching to see what I will do.
Either way, decision-making-time has ended.

Time's up, I jump.

My body tumbles through the once distant, now welcome waters, encompassing me with warmth and energy.

This feels much different than the air I've been breathing.

This feels – alive. I wish they could feel this.

I hope that person who was watching me decides to
    try it too.

I feel like I could stay here for a long, long time,
unaware of my need to breathe.

Aside from the feeling, it's beautiful here,
and my body is able to follow the thoughts of my mind.

In here, they match.

I don't think I've ever matched before now,
didn't even know I should or could.

Rolling onto my back and looking above me,
I see the surface of the water – I can't tell from here
                whether it's rough or not.

From here, it doesn't even matter.
The bellies of the ships above remind me
that someone's waiting – I've got to go.

On the ascent, I'm hopeful that he's there…
    'cuz wasn't he supposed to catch me?

That's what I swore he said…

There is a cold beginning to chase my feet,
you know it – the deep water cold…

the one that makes you feel like you should look
    but if you do, you're wasting what has suddenly
        become very precious time.

I become acutely aware that I don't have even a second
to spare, and my simple ascent becomes an all out race
to break surface.

I pray that he hasn't left me here,
I pray that this is him, above me…

Like a bobber I pop up,
eyes searching for my saving boat…he is not where he
said he would be.

Strike Two.

From here, as the wind begins to kick up the waves
and I'm remembering that I need air to breathe,
that old ship maybe isn't looking so bad…

I calm myself saying if I can't find him, I'll just make
my way back.

Surely someone will help me back up.

One last look around, that's all I need.

Scanning, the other boats are moving around me –
the weather is not agreeing with my decision and the
waves become more aggressive.

"Come on," I ask, "where are you?"

I hear a whistle - turn and there he is,
smiling, inviting me.

"I'm here…waiting for you."

He is a most wonderful sight.
Relief pours over me and I begin to
swim toward him.

This time, I will not take my eyes off him.

I near the point where I can pull myself up,
but he begins to slide away.

> His arms are not rowing, he is drifting,
> always a hair out of my reach –

just enough to give me hope
that my next arm's length will meet the side of his craft.

He does nothing to help me. He pulls the oars inside
his boat and watches me, as I am watching him.

He seems gleefully curious at my effort and the light
smile he wears appears to be at my expense.

I am getting tired.

My arms and legs are growing heavy and this water isn't
as warm as I'd first thought.

It's huge, and there are pockets of cold and warm and
swirls and clouds and currents and undertows
         challenging every move I make.

The sun is eating a hole in my back.

Yet if I roll over for some relief,
I'm afraid I will lose sight of him and be forced back to the rowing and bailing.

Seems the harder I swim, the farther he goes.
Each of my movements, causes him to do the same.

I move toward him, he moves ahead.
I begin to circle around, he does the same.
I stop. So does he.

The waves begin to do the work.
Before I know it, I am at his side.

The boat tips and a wave almost sets me right inside it.

"There is a time," he says, "to trust that all is just as it should be."

His eyes speak to me of peace.
It resonates deep within me and my panic subsides, like the waves.

"Should I just pull myself up?" I ask.

He smiles. "Sure. Just pull yourself up."

I silently question whether or not I will be able to do it and still keep the balance of his small boat,
but just the same my fingers reach up and over the grooved edge,

        I attempt to pull my body up.

The boat begins to tip,
becoming clear that if I do it again,
we will both be treading water with an overturned boat.

He is still smiling.

"How can I get in?" I ask.

He shrugs. "Don't know."

Tiring now, and feeling misled
    I call him on his original call.

"You said you would catch me. You didn't. Now, I am here, stuck in the water and not in any boat. What should I do?"

"When you first jumped, did you enjoy it?"

Remembering the bliss of my body surrounded by the comfort of even-ness, I answer yes.

"But I am tiring now, and would really like to get out of the water. I'm not sure how much longer I can do this."

"I won't leave you," he says.

Without warning the waves begin to pick up,
taking me with them.

My head drops below the surface,
    teasing me with the silence of "under" and the
    noise of "above" in every other second.

I am taking in lung-fulls of water,
choking, blurry eyed, tired.

I still see him here.
He has not left me.

Exhausted now, I am close to going under.
My body is beaten and slow.

I reach out, and with a tired grip,
hold the side of the boat.

He is closer to me now, leaning toward me even.

"How are you doing?" he asks.

Breathless, in a hoarse whisper, I reply. "Kinda tired."

"We have to get you in this boat or you will die."
"I know."
"Then why are you still in the water?"
"Because I can't get in…"

"It's not that you can't. It's that you haven't done it yet."
"How can I?"

"Do you know how I got this boat?
"No."
"I jumped. Just like you."
"How did you get in?"
"I swam in rough waters, just like you."
"Please, I can't hold on much longer. What did you do?"

"I held the side of the boat for just about this amount of time, before it came to me…the one question I had not yet asked…"

"I will die if you do not say quickly what you asked."

Silence.

"Please, what did you ask?"

Utter silence.

    "why won't you help me?"

    "Because you have not asked…"

Council of Warriors

Wanderer, rest here.
Please stop chasing for the day.
I think we live here.

council of warriors
surrounding my skin
tell me the difference
what's out, what's in

not like "in" fashion,
not like "out" doors,
more like "in"-ternal,
yes, internal doors

some open easy,
some will not budge,
warrior council
suggests a slight nudge

so I kick the door open
don't like what I see
can't stand so straight
feel this pressure on me

up from beneath
and down from the top
in from each side
I can't make it stop

blurry, with voices
trembling, whose fear?
shaking, with memory
crying, whose tear?

backing off quickly,
pressure releasing
back to the council
back to their teaching

no kick was needed
I hear them agree
softer, gentler,
introduce these to me

the lessons will come
on this planet, this earth
the rush isn't needed
yet I've done it since birth

a hunger, a longing,
a dream, a quest
each of these feelings
inhaling my chest

understand trade-off
some comes and some goes
working releases in
fingers and toes

let-go-ing some sadness
centuries old
exhaling some fear
that's never been told

couldn't be told
'cuz it's never been met
there are no words for
these memories yet

cellular dancing
lives of their own
each of them holding
what they have known

collective, yet separate
some language spoken,
mostly with feeling,
vibration, unbroken

where have we been
before we formed home?
with this burning question,
do I stand alone?

Heard in Silence

How hungry are you?
Not for food, but to be free.
Search until you are.

When you ask me a question
and silence fills my answer
it is not that
I am holding
you at bay.

At the sound of your voice
I am running back
through doors and jumping through
windows and climbing
over mountains and coming up
from the sands of what
we here call the ocean
and making my way back from
my favorite hiding spot
in the flowers behind the stars
where I've been watching
what goes on down here.

"I know" I am
gaining debt
for things I have not
dealt with yet
but the days between
your voice and my ears
are rough on me
and I've yet to master
this technique of staying
on the earth within this body

but your music
calls me home from home

strengthens me further
with every listen
and through it
I am learning to
be more present in the
meantimes of the times
between your sound

you resonate with me
like the echoes of my angels
and the inspiration
our connection offers
lasts just long enough
to carry me forward
from nightmares and hell-life
in some leaps and bounds
but when my angels get
attacked by those who hate me
I have not fully learned
how
not
to fight for them

these beautiful, beautiful angels
of light are standing by me, loving me,
teaching me, peace-ing me back together
until something maybe I have done
draws attention to them
and I tell them to go away from me
until it is safe for them to come back
in the next century
and they have never listened to me yet

telling me my job is not to protect them
and they stay right where they are
and I prepare to do battle for the
nine millionth time as my angels begin
to get torn apart by every
thing I cannot see but all I can
feel in every moment of all I know,
even to today.

and this is where I will die again as they
are getting blown up, tortured and eaten.

I cannot bear this image or this pain
and for my life so far
I have fought from here
like the ocean storming
under a charcoal black sky
and I don't care that
I've died from here
but mostly I know I have killed from here

as I draw every sword I've
ever owned, every blade
I've ever touched,
they each fit my grip
and become my hands
and those who are pouring
my centuries-old collective wrath
on my radiant angels
covering them with all I cannot
stand to see
pay me in full for my anger
by dying with me as I strike myself down
thinking I have won this time

They are laughing with me as I die,
amused,
enjoying that they will live again
with me on my next go 'round.

I tell them they will not.
They lie down next to me
and touch my face and ooze along
the outside of me as I no longer
let them in
and I watch them tear the wings
and voice away from those I love.

yesterday, my angels
gathered round in spite of my attempts
to chase them away.

I used to question why they kept coming back
knowing as well as I do that
they cannot live here
and my love for them is too great for me
not to die for them
and I have given in to this with some despair
for the first two thousand years
but eventually it became my understanding
that I'd have to enjoy them for the time
that I could
and go to war and die when the time
showed itself again.

many times, the time to die
showed itself through me…
    a guilt I have not shaken yet.

They do not die nicely my angels,
what kills them is not easy.

the last time this happened
one second ago
the angel closest to me spread his
fabulous wings and accepted
an arrow into his chest
as though it had always been there

as I rise up to take that
very same arrow and return it
to its sender with the glory of fire
he drapes himself across my feet
and tells me to be still

there are arrows everywhere
and I am doing all I can to protect
my fallen angel at my feet

No more will touch his preciousness
as long as I am here.

I will absorb it all,
accepting what is coming into me
like it is all I have ever
been deserving of.

I watch the arrows come through
my own chest and
begin to have difficulty swallowing,
with blood on my fingers
I reach down to stroke the
surface of angel dying at my feet

his eyes are so gentle
open or closed his color shines
he is not speaking, only passing
and I am clinging
to the war

as his chest implodes
and the battle comes closer
I wait to meet those
who have again
interfered with our quest for peace

I rest my ear against his
and hear the music of the songs we have danced
to in our earlier form,
the thunder is upon me now
but I have no fear left
my fear is here at my feet
with an arrow through his beauty and truth

I look up to see who haunts me
and as our eyes meet,
there is recognition this time

I see that they are not armed
I see that they are gleeful in my pain and
anxious with anticipation as I consider
in what way they shall die,
understanding of course that so shall I

but they will go first

and maybe they won't follow me back next time

they are not shooting arrows at me
in fact, they are not coming any closer than the surface
of the surface of the surface of my skin

as I will die soon
I have no need for the sword
and so I raise it high above my head
and they circle the blade, inviting me

but instead of giving my gift to them
I bury it deep into the expired
formation of love at my feet
deciding never to draw it again

All is quiet now

those who sought my blade
are slowing down…freezing up…
they appear to be suffering like
the inside of me for a change

it is the inside of me for a change

and all is quiet still

so, my silence is not
formulating some answer.

I am "un-formulating".

This is the stuff
that takes the time.

you ask a question, I look for the answer

Is *that* the truth? No...that's the answer my sociology teacher built...
There...is *that* it? No...that's someone else's answer...
not the one to give today.

not that truth
just *the* truth

I do not want to go
half way with you

I honor and love you

your voice, to me,
is like a calling from home.

a home that is buried lifetimes inside
and on all the vibrations not so
close around me, but getting closer
yet is so, so hard to reach
from here with my feet on the
earth

I have been locking down hatches
getting lost in the woods,
wandering too far out into the ocean,
all to hide from this truth of my memory lanes

I have never been as
truthful with anyone as I have been with you.

not even to my-body-self before now

But you are someone
I cannot afford to pretend with

when I say I love you,
that's me showing up
from beyond the stars

when I say I love you,
I am covering
all of where we've been
and all of where we're going

and when you hugged me
and I touched home for the
first time in this body,
I think you know
I held onto you
for the saving of this life
in that moment

don't worry, I won't burden
you with saving this life.

I'll do that part.

But I will forever
be thankful for the
grounds of us
that makes me
strong enough
to do it

so thank you for your reach

your arms wiped away
a whole lotta stuff,
and I do believe if there was
no schedule to keep
I might ask to stay
tucked in next to you
for the next few
thousand decades or so

and when you placed
your head next to mine
I think you should know
that's the closest I've ever been
to the perfection of the
middle ground
of heaven and earth

you reminded me of
the wing touch of my
closest angel
before the arrows in his chest
kept us from getting too close
as he knew I would wear what
pressed through
forever

he says it's just 'cuz I haven't
learned how to look in the mirror
properly yet

and that they've never been able
to touch me

I just don't fully trust it yet

but that feeling
shared with you
gives me hope
that in this lifetime
the mirror and sleep
won't be such scary
places for me anymore

this is the longest
I've been on the
other side of those walls
and you are the first
I've trusted enough
to explore things here

so, there you have
what goes on in
some of my
silence

thanks for
hearing it out

Healing Yet

how hungry am I?
Searching 'til I drop, I am
famished to be free.

2 am
as I lay here looking
through the pane of this pain
it touches me on a level
of feeling this time

feeling, I think,
is over-rated
in that instant,
I am numbed to it

I get up, stretch,
touch my toes,
smile.

Whew, what a relief.
Glad that's done.

I look out the window
to home
and the stars throw
me a wink.
I miss you too.

2:42 am
someone's tapping on my
forehead.

"do you think that was the answer?"
Uh-oh, I don't think I like this question.
I turn away, pretend I did not hear.

"Where do you suppose
you buried it this time?"
I *really* don't like this question.

I didn't bury it. It has come and gone.
I am better now.

"Really?"

This question has me back
on my knees.
Rolling over onto my back
which is exploding into my guts,
which is raising up to my chest
which has been lying open since
this healing began.

Standing above me
is a vision of light
circling around me
is a vision of light
beneath me, under me,
through me,
all clear.

I recognize that light.
I wore that once.
Until this.

With that a violent rage
kicks up within me,
tearing apart my body
from the inside out

I can barely catch my breath
between lock-ups,
vomit, sweat and chills.

I am so tempted to
lock this all down.
I can, you know.
Just so you all know,
I can swallow this as easy
as my morning vitamin.
I can get out of here…

but as I drag my body
from place to place,
I understand this is not the
answer anymore.

That, is a luxury I can
no longer afford.
Eternity is a really long time
and I will have this as long
as I choose it.

In between my body
tremors, back seizing up,
elbows, shoulders, screaming,
bones creaking, sweating and
puking everything I ever took in,
I am saying, "Thank you. Thank you. Thank you."

4 am
Lying now on my office floor
I am very sore.
I am very tired.
I am worn out.
I am nice.
I cannot see straight.
I cannot see at all.
I close my eyes
and spin with the world.

Interesting.

7 am
It is quieter now.
Maybe I am through the worst of it.
The light continues to circle around me.
Slowly now,
I rise to my knees,
to a Japanese style of sitting.

I look up to the sky,
Yes, I feel better now.
With that comes a new voice.
"Shall we continue?"
"No," I say. "I am done. There is no more.
I am raw."

My head catches fire
and the heat makes me dizzy.
I go back down with the memories
I have buried in my body.

"I am not here to break you down,"
I hear between the crumbling of the inner
walls of me, "I am here to set you free."

"What are you talking about?"

Hands of fire cover my body
and talk to me of the damage I've done.
"You have not respected this body.
You have not once said you loved it.
You have lied to everyone you claim to have loved.
You have loved everyone and everything, more than
yourself.
You are a liar."

I attempt to close my ears
to what I'm hearing
and my chest and head
implode into me.
The ringing is unbearable.
I again begin to choke.

"This, what you are trying to avoid,
is unavoidable. You have an understanding
that is not to be ignored,
least of all, by you. My job with you today is
to help this to be understood."

All of where I've been is lost
All of who I've been is behind me
All of what I sought to ignore is alive with me now

I have been a pretty good liar
in admitting this, pain shoots into my heart and catches
my breath
where it begins
my body is riding through this again
my back closes up, my chest breaks up,
my head closes down,
I am locked

the light is swirling around me

9:48
So there's no other way
but through it
Lying on my back or stomach
or side or rolling or sitting…
I cannot stand 'cuz I'm still with the spinning
there is no comfort
there is nothing to do but puke
and die through it

"No," I hear. "You are not dying again."

From here on the floor
with the sun shining on me
I see the snow on my deck
My overheated body takes
me through the back yard
to feel the energy of our atmosphere
I do not ignore her request

The fire is simmering
with the breath of the breeze

There are two yellow finches
watching me as I pick up the snow
and hold it against my flesh
Our eyes connect one soul
to the other
and I become each,
with their big, little hearts beating
feathers, warming
this one is hungry
I put out some seed
 she is afraid to take it
  I tell her she will feel better if she eats
and she says she can say the same to me

Her wings bring her to where she needs to be
and happily now, she fills her belly

"What do you say about me?"

Her eyes explain my nature to me

"You have piles of food at your feet
and at the tips of each of your fingers and yet
you do not eat.

It is as your friend John said,
you are naked and afraid and have worn everything
but the jacket being offered to you.

You have worn thistles, rockets, bullets, arrows, illness,
heartbreak, rocks, anger, frustration, things that don't
belong to you, things that cannot possibly help you
with what you are to do here, in this life.

You have been a coward…hiding behind some false armor made of anything you could find to cover up your truth. You are like a flame, trying to hide in a house made of straw. You will burn until you are free. You are free to be free."

I ask her if she's cold.

"I keep my feathers on," she says. "Perhaps you should do the same."

With that, the two yellow finches are gone.

10:58
I come back in
with a step a bit lighter
A voice comes to me,
"Getting better now."
My eyes draw up in
search of the source
and my soul draws in
to her old, new empire

I thought maybe I'd gotten
to this point before
and all of hell came back
through the door
so I'm nervous a little
to take the step
but the voice comes again,
saying, "you're not done yet."

My sides are sore, my back is achy,
my eyes are blurry and hands are shaky.
The beating I feel is my very own heart
it's been too long since we've been apart
as I've taken trips away from here
I've left her abandoned, alone with fear
of breaking of crying of loving of dying

I've been concerned with the business of flying
off to the stars where none of this lives
off to the place where everyone gives
freely this love, with no hesitation
it's where I refuel at my favorite station
but on those trips my heart's unguarded
the burning in here is from the fire that started
when I turned my back on this body I'm given
acting like it can just go on living
without my attention, like it doesn't matter
and I've been missing the parts as quickly they scatter
out across these days and nights
keeping stardust in my sights
forgetting that I'm gathering up here
many things that can create fear
forgetting that I need protection
escaping's been my form of heaven
but not to accept responsibly
will clearly be the death of me
and this, I do not wish to see
so this I vow from me to me

11:12
Your efforts are not lost on me
you've offered help where you can see
that I am blind and somewhat broken
hearing me with words unspoken
You've taken me through centuries
where I have had to find some peace
and make amends for where I've been last
and Buddha says I've made it on past
the bits of karma I invited
teaching me how I ignited
living in this form this time
accepting fully what is mine
as finally these dreams are outside
leaving them with nowhere to hide
as once their safest place to be
was here within my memory
buried deep within my body
I can no longer support the party
as I've got lots of work to do
and so do you and me and you

11:59
I raise my hands to touch the light
that advises me to drop the fight
I heed the words I've just been given
and in it comes with the course of Heaven
filling me from head to toe
it's where it's always tried to go
but I've been pushing against its entry
intent on ways that did not suit me
thinking I did not deserve this
like I had the right to say this

when I have always been this light
I've known it throughout all my lives
and finally I come to see
that I am light and light is me

I play hard this game called life
I do not always do what's right
but now I have experience
to take your hand and also a chance
and I am done impeding progress
and I am standing now with promise
that I will honor what I have here
I will cherish what I am here
most of all, I'll come to you,
the truth of me I'll offer you,
I had to take this one last journey
to help me have the eyes to see
to help me have the heart to feel
to help me understand I'm real
to help me say I could use some help please
to accept it then, and to try and not freeze
but to open up the light of me
to let it live, to set it free,
this is what I've come to see
as I have journeyed down through me.

1:19
Motionless now, body resting,
soul to God, is this like nesting?
This is how you rest yourself
This is how you love yourself

I close my eyes with inner peace
I breathe in from the sun
and out through the trees
There is a gem of a universe
it's here, in my heart, you polished it first
I'd offer it to you in velvet wrap
but it would kill me in a second flat
and I love us too much to put us through that,
so I'll keep it here, safe where it's at
and I'll polish it often,
I promise you that.

I see you here, from where I lay,
you look really great today…
your beauty is awesome I really must say
and thank you for helping me through today

The ache I'm left with is a soft reminder
of where I will be if I fall behind-er
forward's a better direction for us
thanks for helping me find this trust
to touch the love that humbles me

echoing eternally,
love to me to you to me,
this is enough to make me free,

it's all there is,

        I finally see.

ABOUT THE AUTHOR

Michelle grew up in Chicago, the youngest of 7 and fortunate enough to be raised by one who encouraged exploration and growth in all directions. At a young age, she began writing, influenced by things around her, both visible and non-visible.
Treasured experiences built an interest in the exploration of life and spirit energy through many avenues. These studies and pursuits continue through her practice of Aikido and Traditional Chinese Medicine.
Michelle is a licensed acupuncturist and practitioner in a clinic she co-founded, Acupuncture & Oriental Medicine, located in Illinois. She is also an instructor of Aikido at the Abiding Spirit Center and the Aikido Shimboku Kai.

Made in the USA
Charleston, SC
18 September 2012